CASTLES IN WALES

CASTLES IN WALES

Rebecca King

DIAL HOUSE

First published 1996

ISBN 0 7110 2422 7

© Ian Allan Publishing 1996

Published by Dial House

an imprint of Ian Allan Ltd, Terminal House, Station Approach, Shepperton, Surrey TW17 8AS. Printed by Ian Allan Printing Ltd, Coombelands House, Coombelands Lane, Addlestone, Surrey KT15 1HY.

All photographs supplied courtesy of Wales Tourist Board except for those on pages 4, 17, 26 and 75, supplied by the AA Picture Library.

Front cover:
Pembroke Castle, Dyfed
Dominated by its massive castle, the town of Pembroke sits on the southern side of the tidal Pembroke River, part of the huge Milford Haven waterway.

Back cover and right:
Dolbadarn Castle, Gwynedd
Visitors are drawn to the few remains of this native Welsh castle because of the beauty of its position: Turner came here to paint the scene.

Previous page:
Denbigh Castle, Clwyd
Prior to Edward's castle at Denbigh, a fortress built by Llewelyn the Last's brother occupied this advantageous site above the Clwyd River, the former Welsh/English border.

Far right:
Caerphilly Castle, Mid Glamorgan
A snowy scene at Caerphilly Castle.

Introduction

From romantic hilltop ruins to huge multi-towered fortresses, from fortified manor houses to glorious 19th-century shams, castles are part of the very fabric and history of Wales.

Today they are preserved and trumpeted as a range of tourist attractions, but in reality the castles in Wales are lasting monuments to the power struggle that waged between Wales and England for five centuries.

The story of castles begins with the Normans. Having stormed through England and killed King Harold at the Battle of Hastings, William established a chain of barons, the Lords Marcher (*marche* means frontier in French) along the Welsh border. Their role was to gain control of as much Welsh territory as they could, and to this end numerous earth and timber (motte and bailey) structures were thrown up. A stone castle was built at Chepstow in 1067, but this was the exception and only into the 12th century was the use of stone widespread. Sometimes stone castles replaced the earlier wooden structures, sometimes they were built on new sites.

With the reign of Henry II (1154–89) came a period of uneasy truce, and the Welsh rulers were able to consolidate their position. Taking their cue from the Normans, they began to build stone castles of their own in the west and north particularly. One of these powerful rulers was Llywelyn the Great (1173–1240) and as his strength grew, more powerful attacks were made on the Marcher strongholds. It soon became clear that greater defences were necessary if the English were to maintain their control. Thus the great round-towered castles with massive curtain walls, such as Pembroke

and Skenfrith, appeared in the English lordships.

After Llywelyn's death in 1240 it was his grandson, Llywelyn the Last, who emerged as the new leader in Wales. Henry III was under threat from his barons, led by Simon de Montfort, and Llywelyn was acknowledged as Prince of Wales by the Treaty of Montgomery in 1267. This prompted more building and reinforcement on the borders, and castles such as Caerphilly were begun.

Meanwhile, in turn, the castles of Llywelyn the Great were being fortified by his grandson against a background of increasing hostility with the new king of England, Edward I. Llywelyn refused to comply with the

agreements made in the Treaty of Montgomery and Edward was finally spurred into taking decisive action. Thus began the first wave of the huge programme of castle-building in North Wales that was to see the construction of some of Europe's finest medieval military strongholds. While these great towers and curtain walls were being raised, Edward was busy reinforcing his power over the rest of Wales; instructing his Marcher lords to take control of as much land as possible. Inevitably this led to revolt among the Welsh people, who looked to Llywelyn as their patriotic leader. Attacks and counter-attacks followed, but when the prince was killed in 1282 it was as if the death-knell of Welsh independence had been sounded.

Edward, determined to conquer the country once and for all, had begun building another batch of castles and also instigated the repair of many former Welsh strongholds. A last-ditch attempt by Madog ap Llywelyn in 1294 to lead an uprising was soon quelled, but its occurrence was enough to prompt Edward into building his final and possibly greatest castle, Beaumaris, before he turned his attention abroad.

With the final subjugation of the Welsh, castle-building was no longer a priority and over the next century of relative peace many castles made the transition from fortress to country residence, and thus the fortified manor house emerged.

The spirit of Welsh independence had not been completely crushed, however, and at the end of the 14th century a new Welsh leader appeared on the scene, Owain Glyndwr. In the revolt he took Harlech and Aberystwyth and in doing so the Welsh once again became a force to be reckoned with, but it was due to the strength of Edward's fortresses that they did not gain a greater hold. In about 1408 Harry of Monmouth (Henry V) retook the castles and Glyndwr's revolt seemed to fade away.

During the prosperous Tudor era many minor castles had been turned into sumptuous country mansions, but with the advent of the Civil War between Charles I and Parliament in 1642 the castle once again came into its own as a fortification. Virtually the whole of Wales supported King Charles in the Royalist cause and so many castles were garrisoned against the Parliamentarians. As a result several were 'slighted', ie blown up with gunpowder, and it was this which accounts for a good number of the ruins seen today.

So ends the real story of the castle in Wales, but there is one other phase of building that has a place in the picture. The Industrial Revolution had a massive impact on Wales and towards the end of the 18th century huge fortunes were being amassed by entrepreneurs in the coal and slate industries. Wanting to symbolise their wealth and status, these magnates built glorious mock castles in the manner of their Norman and medieval counterparts which, although 'sham', are every bit as remarkable as their predecessors.

Above:

Abergavenny Castle, Gwent
South of Abergavenny town centre

Standing in a public park south of Abergavenny are the ruins of a castle that once belonged to William de Braose. This unpleasant Norman lord is said to have invited various Welsh dignitaries to the castle for a feast, with the sole intention of murdering them, which he promptly did. De Braose got his comeuppance, however, as later the castle was sacked by the Welsh and the ruthless King John took his family to Windsor Castle where they were starved to death.

Most of the stonework that remains today dates from the 13th and 14th centuries, although the remnants of the curtain walls are probably earlier. The folly at the top of the mound was built in the 19th century.

Above:

Aberystwyth Castle, Dyfed

Aberystwyth seafront

This was one of the first castles to be built by Edward I in Wales, albeit on a smaller scale than those at Conwy or Caernarfon, for example. Standing above the promenade on the headland at the point where the River Rheidol flows into Cardigan Bay, Aberystwyth was built to a kind of double diamond plan. Owain Glyndwr captured it in 1404, but after four years Prince Henry (Henry V) managed to take it back. During the Civil War in the 17th century it was finally blown up by the Parliamentarians after the Royalist garrison had surrendered.

Left, below and right:

Beaumaris Castle, Gwynedd

Beaumaris, Isle of Anglesey

Claimed to be the perfect concentric castle, Beaumaris was both the last and the largest of Edward I's mighty fortresses. Its architect was the master mason James of St George who had gained some fame for his work both in Wales and on the Continent.

From the air it is possible to appreciate the precise symmetry of the design and identify the 'rings' of defences which gave rise to the term concentric. The first line was the moat, about 18ft in width, with a tidal dock at the southern end, so ships laden with supplies could sail right up to the main gate. The next line of defence was the low curtain wall with its 16 towers and two gateways. Then came the high walls and six great towers which protected the inner ward.

Entry to this is through the two huge gatehouses which would have had various state rooms attached to them had the castle ever been finished. It was also intended that spacious domestic buildings be erected in the inner ward, but within three years of the first stone being laid in 1205, funds had dried up. By this time the king's interests lay elsewhere and so the full potential of Beaumaris was never realised. Nevertheless, with its commanding views of the Menai Strait, this sophisticated example of military architecture stands as one of the great castles of Wales.

Right and far right:
Beaupre Castle, South Glamorgan
Near Cowbridge

Quietly tucked away in the Vale of Glamorgan are the remains of this mainly Elizabethan manor house. Its name, derived from *beau-repaire*, means beautiful retreat and is as apt a label today as it was in Norman times when a residence of some kind was first established on the site. The titled Basset family later occupied the house and it is Sir Richard's coat of arms that can be seen carved above the doorway. Substantial remains of the two chief building periods, the 14th and 16th centuries, can be seen.

Left and right:
Bodelwyddan Castle, Clwyd
Bodelwyddan, west of St Asaph

A castle in name only, this castellated mansion with its turrets owes its appearance to 19th-century remodelling. There has, however, been a house on the site for considerably longer than this. Records date back to the 1460s, and an Elizabethan building was refashioned in a neo-classical style right at the beginning of the 19th century. A few years later it assumed its present guise.

Having been taken in hand by Clwyd County Council, this is now the home of important Victorian collections from the National Portrait Gallery, the Victoria and Albert Museum and the Royal Academy of Art. Various Victorian exhibitions and amusements are also featured. Seen here is the great hall with its plaster vaulting. Outside, there are lovely gardens, a maze, an aviary and woodland walks.

Caernarfon Castle, Gwynedd
Western edge of Caernarfon

As well as being a mighty fortress, Caernarfon was built by Edward I to be a palace fit for royalty and a seat of government for the newly-formed counties of North Wales. The king's son, Edward of Caernarfon, the first English Prince of Wales, was born here in 1284. Thus there is a splendour about the residential accommodation that sets Caernarfon apart from Edward's other great castles.

However, the castle never really fulfilled the role it was built for and, having surrendered to Parliamentary forces in the mid-17th century, fell into disrepair. Not until the late 19th century when Anthony Salvin was commissioned to restored the stonework did Caernarfon's fortunes take an upturn. From then on refurbishment continued apace and by the early 20th century it once again became a place fit for princes: Edward (later Edward VIII) was invested here in 1911, as was Prince Charles in 1969, with due pomp and ceremony.

Exhibitions, displays and museums all add to the interest of a visit here.

Left:
View across the River Seiont.

Above:
The upper and lower wards from the Eagle Tower.

17

Above and right:

Caerphilly Castle, Mid Glamorgan

Caerphilly town centre

One of the most striking features about Caerphilly is its enormous size: altogether, it covers some 30 acres.

The Romans were the first to recognise the strategic importance of the site and established a fort here in AD75. However, it was not until the mid-13th century that the existing castle was begun by Gilbert de Clare, a Marcher lord, to defend his land from Llywelyn ap Gruffydd, the last native Prince of Wales.

Built to a concentric design with enormous gatehouses and towers surrounded by a huge lake, Caerphilly is one of the greatest surviving medieval castles in Europe. In the late 19th century the wealthy third Marquess of Bute (and later his son) extensively restored the complex after it had suffered centuries of neglect.

Now, there is an exhibition in the outer gatehouse, boat trips are available on the lake and various re-enactment events are held on the site.

Caldicot Castle, Gwent
South-west of Chepstow

Built by the Normans as one of the Marcher castles, Caldicot was substantially rebuilt by Joseph R. Cobb, a wealthy Victorian barrister and antiquary. (Cobb acquired various Welsh castles during his lifetime, including Pembroke and Manorbier.)

Of the original parts, the 14th-century gatehouse and round tower are the most impressive. These were built by Thomas Woodcock, sixth son of Edward III. Medieval banquets are held in the great hall of the gatehouse and there are exhibitions of local history, plus pretty gardens.

Cardiff Castle, South Glamorgan
Cardiff city centre

In the north-west corner of the castle grounds, set apart from the Victorian domestic buildings, is the shell of the Norman keep. Built on the site of the Roman defences, which covered an eight-acre site, it began as a wooden palisade. By the end of the 12th century, however, the 12-sided stone building seen today had been erected. Within another 100 years or so, further strengthening was necessary. In the 15th century a gatehouse was added.

In the 18th century Cardiff Castle became the property, through marriage, of the Bute family, who helped transform the town into a major port.

When the third Marquess (reputed to be the richest man in Britain at the time) inherited the castle in the 19th century he decided to transform it — the Gothic concoction that makes up the bulk of what we see today is the result of his collaboration with William Burges — medievalist, architect and sometime opium smoker.

Bute and Burges shared a passion for religious art and the symbolism of the Middle Ages and no expense was spared in executing their flights of fancy. Throughout, the rooms are a kaleidoscope of intense colour and extraordinary design, with much allegory and medieval allusion.

The 150ft-high Clock Tower, at the corner of the castle, was just one of Bute's additions to the original simple buildings. Painted statues of the planets adorn the outside, while inside are the Summer and Winter Smoking Rooms and the Bachelors' Bedroom.

Distinctive too is the Octagonal Tower with its wooden spire.

Cardiff Castle, South Glamorgan
Cardiff city centre
Left:
The Clock Tower.

Right
The castle towers from Bute Park.

Right:
Cardiff Castle, South Glamorgan
Cardiff city centre
The interior of Cardiff Castle.

Above:
Carew, Dyfed
East of Pembroke

Set above the tidal River Carew with meadows on either side, the castle has evolved over the centuries from the original stone building that replaced the simple Norman motte and bailey. In the 15th century, a relatively peaceful period in Wales's history, it was considerably enlarged and transformed into a handsome Tudor house.

Near the entrance is Carew Cross, a fine 11th-century cross standing nearly 14ft high.

Above:
Carreg Cennen, Dyfed
South-east of Llandeilo

Superbly sited high above the Cennen valley right on the edge of a huge limestone bluff, the natural advantages of Carreg Cennen's position are clear to see. Like Edward's concentric castles in North Wales, the design here is based on a series of defences within each other. Built as a Welsh stronghold, it was partially destroyed by the Earl of Pembroke in 1462.

From the inner ward a narrow passage leads along the cliff face to a cave known from findings of skeletons to be occupied during prehistoric times.

Above:
Castell y Bere, Gwynedd
North of Abergynolwyn

The ruins of this former Welsh stronghold lie deep in the heart of Wales on a rocky outcrop in the upper Dysynni valley. Towering above it is the mass of Cader Idris. This was one of Llywelyn the Great's castles, but it was taken by Edward I's men in 1283 and later abandoned. The beauty of the castle — of which there are scant remains — lies in its isolation and spectacular setting.

Left and right:
Castell Coch, South Glamorgan
North-west of Cardiff

When first glimpsed above the trees on a steep hillside above the Taff valley, Castell Coch looks all the world like something out of a fairytale. In reality, it is another amazing extravaganza created by William Burges and Lord Bute (see page 21). Work on Cardiff Castle had already begun when Bute decided he wanted a country retreat to complement it, and commissioned Burges to draw up plans. Sadly, Burges died suddenly in 1881 and completion of the decoration took another ten years.

Here, too, the brilliant and eccentric pair's taste for religion and the Middle Ages is evident. Inside is an explosion of fantasy and fable. The dining room (*right*) has a glorious vaulted ceiling decorated with birds and butterflies, and murals depicting scenes from Aesop's Fables adorn the walls. Portraits of members of the Bute family strike a rather more sombre note. The other rooms are equally stunning; a riot of mythology, symbolism and humour.

Chepstow Castle, Gwent
Chepstow

Chepstow was built on the banks of the River Wye to guard the route into Wales from southern England. It is believed to be the first castle to be built of stone in Wales, the great tower keep dating from 1067, just a year after William's victory at Hastings. William created Marcher lordships to subdue the Welsh and expand into their territory and over the next 200 years increasingly powerful fortifications had to be maintained for this purpose Chepstow was no exception and underwent several phases of expansion.

The castle consists of three enclosures. The lower ward, dating from the 13th century, is the largest with an exhibition in the great hall. Separated from this by 12th-century defences is the middle ward where the ruins of the great tower still stand. Beyond this is the upper ward which leads up to the barbican watch tower (*right*). From here there are superb views over the castle complex, the town and the river estuary.

Right and far right:
Chirk Castle, Clwyd
Just west of Chirk

Unlike many of its contemporaries, this former border fortress, completed in 1310, is now an elegant stately home rather than a romantic ruin. Externally, with its drum corner towers, it resembles other Edwardian castles, but inside fine furniture, portraits, carving and decoration fill the spacious rooms, reflecting the tastes and fashions from the 16th to the 19th centuries.

English architect A. W. N. Pugin (1812-52) carried out many unsatisfactory alterations here in the 1840s, but since then several rooms have been restored to their original states. Beautiful ornamental gardens make up part of the huge parkland estate.

Chirk Castle, Clwyd
Just west of Chirk

Among Chirk's notable features are the wrought-iron gates now marking the entrance to the estate: originally they stood on the north side. Made in about 1720 by two local blacksmiths, Robert and Thomas Davies of Bersham, near Wrexham, the gates are regarded as a particularly fine example of the period. They bear the Myddleton family's coat of arms, who have occupied the castle since the late 16th century.

Cilgerran Castle, Dyfed
South of Cardigan

Above:

Popular legend has it that Nest, the 'Welsh Helen of Troy', was abducted here in the 12th century by Prince Owain of Powys, who had fallen in love with her. In the attack he set not only the castle but the whole of Wales on fire. This seems unlikely, but the original earth and timber structure was certainly destroyed at some point, the stone castle seen today dating from the 13th century.

Two huge round towers, originally four storeys high, still dominate the site and because of its location above the River Teifi it became a favourite subject with artists during the 18th and 19th centuries.

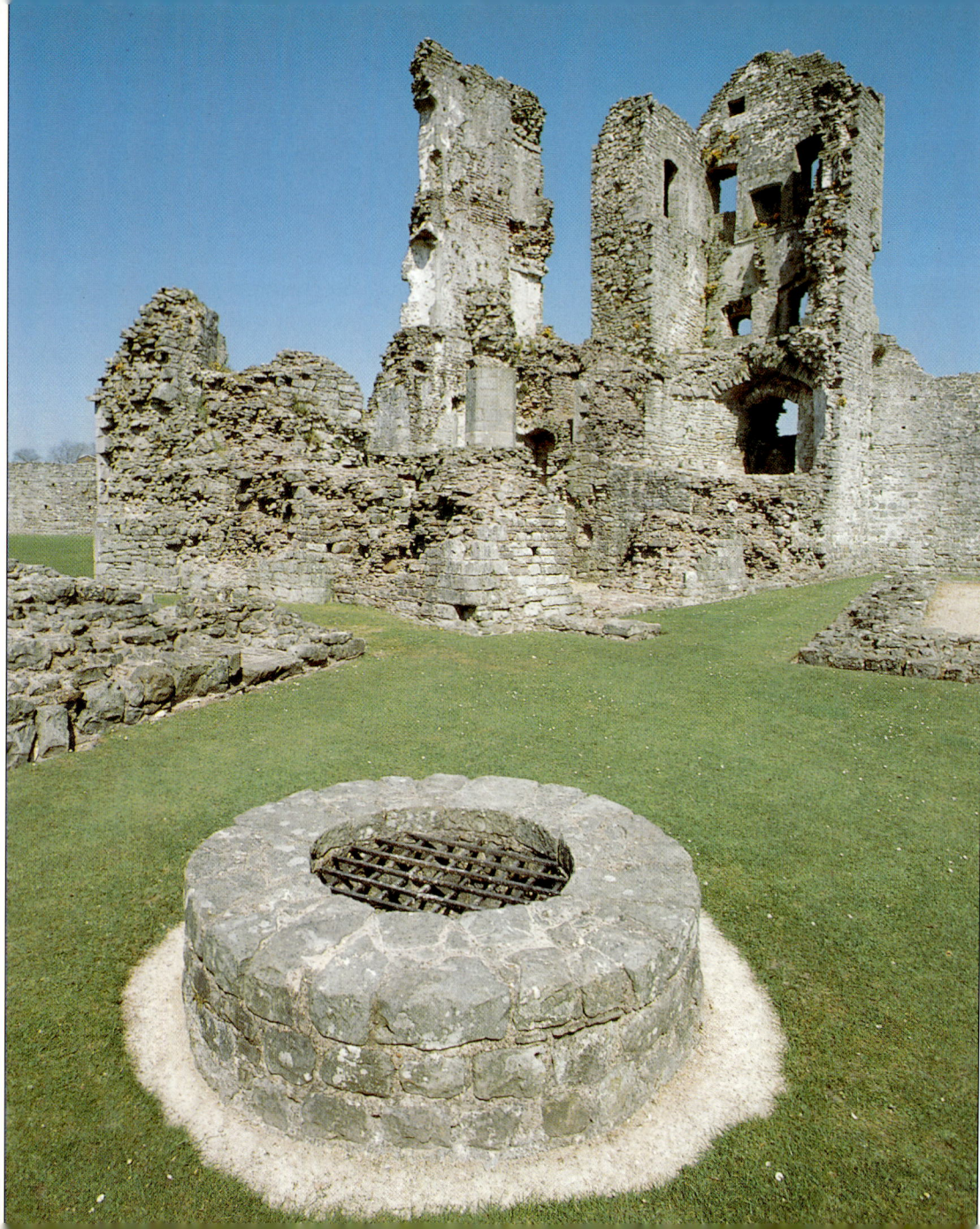

Right and far right:

Coity Castle, Mid Glamorgan

North-east of Bridgend

Like many other Welsh castles, Coity began life as a timber and earthwork motte and bailey. It was not until the late 12th century that a stone building was constructed, although the ruins seen today in fact are the remains of major remodelling in the 14th century.

Originally a Norman lordship belonging to the Turbervilles, the surrounding land was acquired without battle as the heir married the heiress of the former Welsh lord.

During the Welsh uprising under Owain Glyndwr, Coity withstood a long siege, eventually falling into decay in the 16th century when the male line died out.

Above and right:

Conwy Castle, Gwynedd
Conwy

It was not until his second campaign in Wales that Edward I took control of the Conwy valley, but, having done so, he lost no time in building a new fortress and garrison town to go with it. Within just five years the castle and town walls were thrown up at the mouth of the River Conwy under the direction of James of St George, Edward's favourite architect.

Linear rather than concentric in design because of the nature of the terrain, the castle consists of eight enormous towers set in a rectangle around two wards. These were separated by a drawbridge and turrets so the inner ward could still be defended if the outer ward fell. Although mostly roofless, the great hall and king's apartments are well preserved. The town walls, 30ft high with 21 evenly spaced towers, are also very well preserved.

Today, three bridges span the river by the castle: Thomas Telford's suspension bridge of 1826; George Stephenson's railway bridge carrying the London-to-Holyhead line; and the modern road bridge.

Above and right:

Criccieth Castle, Gwynedd

West of Porthmadog

The castle commanding the coastline from its hilltop perch above the quiet seaside resort of Criccieth was probably first built by Llywelyn the Great in the early 13th century.

Having fallen to Edward I in 1283, it was subsequently altered and strengthened over the years and withstood various attacks. One of the latest additions was the rectangular Engine Tower at the northern end of the castle. During the 1404 rebellion the castle was finally regained by the Welsh, only to be abandoned and left to fall into ruin.

There is an exhibition on Welsh castles and their history on the site.

Above:
Denbigh Castle, Clwyd
Denbigh
The castle ruins tower above the town of Denbigh in the Vale of Clwyd, the old town walls scattered on the hillside below. Most impressive of these hilltop remnants is the gatehouse which consisted of three octagonal towers, seen here from inside the castle.

Dolbadarn Castle, Gwynedd
South-east of Llanberis
The beauty of Dolbadarn Castle lies in its glorious position overlooking Llyn Padarn at the northern edge of Snowdonia. Thought to be built by Llywelyn the Great, the 40ft-high round keep still stands guard over the Llanberis Pass.

Above:

Dolwyddelan Castle, Gwynedd
Dolwyddelan
This remote spot midway between Blaenau Ffestiniog and Betws-y-Coed is generally held to be the birthplace of the Welsh prince, Llywelyn the Great. Probably built by his father at the end of the 12th century, the castle was taken by Edward 1 and used to subdue the Welsh. For centuries it has stood abandoned, although the battlements and wall walks were reconstructed in Victorian times.

Above:
Flint Castle, Clwyd
Flint

Just a few minutes' walk from the town centre lie the sandstone ruins of Flint Castle, built by Edward I to guard the coastal marshes of the Dee estuary and the shipping lanes into the then important port of Chester. It was the first of the castles in what became known as the Iron Ring: the huge fortresses built around the north coast during the king's struggles with Llywelyn the Last. Like all the castles of James of St George, Flint formed part of a bastide town. Inhabited by English settlers, these walled enclaves did not allow the Welsh to trade in them or to enter them carrying arms.

Above:

Grosmont Castle, Gwent

North-west of Monmouth

Set right on the English border, on a small hill above the village, are the ruins of Grosmont Castle. Together with Skenfrith and White castles, it formed the once-impressive trio called the Three Castles. Lying within an eight-mile radius of each other, they were built to protect this accessible region of the turbulent Marcher lands. Not until 1902 did they come under separate ownership. Of the three, Grosmont has fared the worst.

Left and above:

Gwrych Castle, Clwyd

West of Abergele

One of the mock medieval castles created in the 19th century to reflect their owners' prosperity and status, Gwrych was the work of a wealthy Lancastrian, Bamford Hesketh. The fashion at the time was to recall the Romantic Movement and the style of the Middle Ages as elaborately as possible, thus castellations, gothic windows and false towers were all lavishly employed. Inspiration was undoubtedly drawn from nearby Conwy Castle, further west along the coast.

Seen here are the stables and the window in the hall.

47

Left and above:

Harlech Castle, Gwynedd

Harlech

Built of Harlech grit, the hard Cambrian rock on which it stands, this mighty castle seems to grow out of the cliff face. It was begun during Edward's second campaign in North Wales and is another component of the famous Iron Ring. Perched on its 200ft-high bluff with the sea directly below it (the shoreline has since receded), the castle was vulnerable from the east only and its first line of defence here was the massive and formidable gatehouse (*left*). Remarkable, too, is the fortified route down the cliff face to the sea which gave access to supplies arriving by boat.

Entitled *The Two Kings*, the modern statue outside the castle (*above*) represents an episode from a collection of Welsh folk tales called The Mabinogion. Transcribed in medieval times, they are concerned, among other things, with Celtic mythology, life and death, historical events, Arthurian legends and the underworld. Many of the stories have precise geographical settings which can be traced today.

Haverfordwest Castle, Dyfed

Haverfordwest

Gilbert de Clare, the powerful 12th-century Earl of Pembroke, chose to build one of his castles on this strategic site 80ft above the River Cleddau. The town which grew around it is still dominated by the ruins. Unfortunately, there is little here to see of the fortification other than the shell of the inner ward, but a museum is housed in the former prison next door.

Kidwelly Castle, Dyfed

Kidwelly

There are marvellous views over the coastline of Carmarthen Bay from Kidwelly, which is chiefly why the spot was chosen in the first place. Together with a priory (long gone), the castle was initially built at the beginning of the 12th century by the Bishop of Salisbury as a satellite of Sherborne Abbey in Dorset. It was much altered and extended in medieval times, but since then has remained relatively untouched and the fine ruins are remarkably well preserved.

51

Above:

Laugharne Castle, Dyfed
Laugharne

Such is the beauty of the setting of Laugharne Castle on the banks of the peaceful Taf estuary that J. M. W. Turner chose it as the subject of one his paintings. Since those days the ivy-clad ruins have been extensively restored and were reopened to the public in 1995. The village draws thousands of visitors each year because of its associations with the poet Dylan Thomas. He lived here for four years before his death in 1953. His house can be visited.

Above:

Llanstephan Castle, Dyfed

South-west of Carmarthen

In about 600BC an Iron Age promontory fort occupied the headland on which Llanstephan Castle stands, which gives some clue to the views it commands. The twin-towered gatehouse, built around 1280, became the main living quarters of the castle and in Tudor times was converted into a house. A large sandy beach stretches out below.

Right and far right:
Manorbier Castle, Dyfed
South-west of Tenby

Founded in the 12th century by a powerful Norman family, Manorbier's main claim to fame is as the birthplace of Giraldus Cambrensis, Gerald of Wales.

Gerald, a scholar-cum-preacher, travelled throughout the country delivering sermons and recruiting for the third Crusade. As he did so he gathered material about the landscape and the people which was subsequently published in two books, The Journey Through Wales and The Description of Wales. They provide a unique insight into medieval life in Wales.

The castle, perched on its gorse-covered hill overlooking the village's quiet beach, is in a good state of repair. Never seriously attacked, it served mainly as a comfortable country residence. The baronial hall and state apartment are still in evidence.

Right:
Newcastle Emlyn Castle, Dyfed
South-east of Cardigan
A great loop of the River Teifi surrounds these picturesque ruins in the heartland of agricultural Wales. Built by the Welsh (it was the only stone castle they did build in this region), Newcastle Emlyn was always more of a country residence than a military fortress. It was finally blown up during the Civil War.

Ogmore, Mid Glamorgan

South-west of Bridgend

Unusually for a Norman castle, Ogmore is sited at the bottom of a valley rather than on top of a hill. The explanation for this is that it was built to guard an important crossing point on the River Ewenny. Like many of these early castles, it acquired a stone keep and was further added to in the 13th century.

Above:

Oxwich Castle, West Glamorgan
South-west of Swansea

The manor house built here in the 16th century probably took its name from a castle that originally stood on the site. Houses of this period occupied by the gentry were extremely substantial, often reflecting past medieval grandeur and design. The remains show that Oxwich boasted a long gallery, a six-storey high tower and a great hall.

Oystermouth Castle, West Glamorgan
South-west of Swansea

Looming over the seaside sprawl of Oystermouth, overlooking Swansea Bay, are the ruins of the castle founded by the Normans as a watch tower. Further strengthening took place later as defence against the Welsh, and in the 14th century it was altered to become a residence of some standing. The ruins are impressive, still standing to their original height, with state rooms and a banqueting hall.

Right and far right:
Pembroke Castle, Dyfed
Pembroke

Clearly the most impressive part of Pembroke Castle still standing is the round Norman keep, 75ft high and capped by a dome. From the top there are magnificent views over Milford Haven.

This was one of the Norman lords' greatest strongholds and, completely rebuilt in the 12th and 13th centuries, was never overtaken by the Welsh. It formed part of the military chain across Pembrokeshire that kept them at bay.

During the Civil War it started out as a Parliamentarian stronghold (the only one in south Wales), but the town's governor made a political about-turn in support of the king, Charles I, and Cromwell consequently sacked the castle. Despite the onslaught, the remains are still impressive.

A unique feature of the castle is that it is built over a huge natural cavern. Called the Wogan, this is reached by steps leading down from the hall.

Above and right:

Penhow Castle, Gwent

East of Newport

This fortified manor house, consisting of a haphazard collection of buildings dating from the 12th to the 15th centuries, claims to be the oldest inhabited castle in Wales. The oldest part is the three-storey square keep, the original fortification was linked to nearby Chepstow Castle. Shown above is the 14th-century gatehouse.

Inside the 15th-century great hall (*right*), decorating the edge of the minstrels' gallery are the arms (a pair of wings) of the Seymour family who lived here. After the male line died out at the end of the 15th century the house passed to the Bowles family, who built this part. A third wing was built in Tudor times by the subsequent owner, Thomas Lewis. Tours take visitors round in chronological order.

Right and far right:

Penrhyn Castle, Gwynedd

East of Bangor

Wealth created by the slate industry in North Wales during the 19th century built this extraordinary neo-Norman pile overlooking the Menai Strait. Created by architect Thomas Hopper, the house, which includes a great four-storey keep, is said to be the most outstanding example of Norman revival in Britain. This is opulence and ostentation on a grand scale, with something over 300 rooms lavishly decorated in more-or-less Romanesque style. Slate also features throughout the house, including items such as a full-size billiard table and a bed weighing about a ton, designed for Queen Victoria .

A Victorian garden, woodland, an industrial railway (constructed to take the slate down to the port built to the northeast of Bangor by the Pennant family, former owners of the castle) and a railway museum also form part of this National Trust property.

Above:

Picton Castle, Dyfed

South-east of Haverfordwest

Glorious grounds with far-reaching views over the Cleddau valleys surround this rather severe castle. The older part of the building, with four round towers, was built in the days of Edward I, while a new four-storey extension was added on at the beginning of the 19th century.

A feature here is the gallery of paintings by Graham Sutherland (1903—80) which now occupies the stables.

Right:

Powis Castle, Powys

Just south of Welshpool

The magnificent red gritstone building that we see today largely dates from Elizabethan times. Onetime seat of Welsh princes, the castle became English property after the owners switched their allegiance in return for a baronetcy. A huge building programme followed, then later, in the 16th century, further extensive refurbishment was made. Numerous elegant rooms inside are filled with fine furniture and paintings, and the Clive of India Museum contains a range of objects brought back from India.

The gardens, cascading down to the River Severn in four huge terraces, are the work of 18th-century Welsh architect, William Winde.

Above:
Raglan Castle, Gwent
South-west of Monmouth
Although it bears some of the hallmarks of Edward's great castles, Raglan was not begun until the 15th century; it claims to the last medieval fortification to be built in Britain. The great tower, surrounded by a moat, is hexagonal in design with a series of complex drawbridges. Above the moat walk, on 12ft-high walls, is the bowling green.

Rhuddlan Castle, Clwyd
South of Rhyl

A canalised section of the River Clwyd now provides the ruins of Rhuddlan Castle with a beautiful setting, but its original purpose was to connect the castle with the sea some two miles away. This allowed ships to bring supplies to the castle and provided water for the huge moat. Gillot's Tower, down by the river, protected the dock.

The castle was built during Edward's first campaign in Wales by James of St George and became famous as the place where the king signed the Statute of Rhuddlan on 19 March 1284. This, also known as the Great Statute of Wales, laid down the laws under which Wales should be governed.

Right:
Roch Castle, Dyfed
South-east of Newgale
The D-shaped tower of the original castle stands on a rocky outcrop, from which it takes its name. There is a rather fanciful legend that Adam de la Roche chose this site because he had a phobia about snakes, but as luck would have it, an adder was brought into the castle with some firewood and bit the luckless Adam, who died as a result. During reconstruction at the turn of the 20th century, a modern wing was added,

Above:

Skenfrith Castle, Gwent

North-east of Abergavenny

Along with Grosmont and White castles, Skenfrith is one of the Three Castles that controlled the routes into Wales between the riverside cliffs of the Wye valley and the Black Mountains. It stands by the River Monnow, with its 21ft-high keep raised on a small mound still standing in the centre of the ward. Round towers stood at the four corners of this rectangle.

71

Above:
Swansea Castle, West Glamorgan
Swansea
Not all of Wales's castles stand romantically amid beautiful scenery: Swansea, for example, is surrounded by modern shopping developments near the city centre.

The Normans raised one of their first earth and timber motte and bailey castles here in the 11th century, later to be replaced with the stone building which remains. The chief feature here is the arcaded parapet around the upper walls, thought possibly to be the work of Henry de Gowr, bishop of St David's.

Right:

Tenby Castle, Dyfed

Tenby

From their headland site the ruins of Tenby's castle overlook the town and harbour of this popular Pembrokeshire holiday resort. Built by the Normans as part of their plan to make a 'Little England Beyond Wales', the castle was strengthened after repeated attacks by the Welsh. This additional fortification included building town walls, and these remain as the most complete circuit in South Wales. Only one of the four entrance gates remain, however – the west gate.

Above:
Tretower Castle, Powys
North-west of Crickhowell
During the 13th century the round keep that makes such a conspicuous landmark today was raised to replace an earlier fortification. Later, a more spacious manor house, Tretower Court, was built near by, which was further added to in the 15th century. Now restored, these buildings evoke something of the feeling of medieval life and their construction provides an insight into building methods of the time.

Above:
Weobley Castle, West Glamorgan
West of Gowerton

Here is another of South Wales's fortified manor houses, built initially as a defensive fortification then gradually added to and altered over the years to provide gracious accommodation fit for nobility. Romantically set above the Llanrhidian marshes on the Gower peninsula, visitors come here as much for the scenic setting as the remains themselves.

Above and right:

White Castle, Gwent

Llantilio Crossenny, east of Abergavenny

The most impressive of Gwent's Three Castles (see Grosmont and Skenfrith), White Castle commands fine views across open countryside to the Skirrid mountain. It takes its name from the simple fact that it was rendered with white plaster at one time, but only traces of this can be seen now.

From the outer ward, enclosed by a curtain wall and protected by four towers, visitors cross the bridge spanning the deep moat to enter the inner ward. Two great towers form the inner gatehouse, one of which can be climbed: the views from the top are well worth the effort.

Above:

Manorbier Castle, Dyfed

South-west of Tenby

Another view of the castle perched on its gorse-covered hill.

Many of the castles in Wales are either in the care of Cadw: Welsh Historic Monuments, or the National Trust. Membership of both can be obtained. Some castles mentioned in this book are privately owned, but open to visitors on a regular basis. A few can be viewed only from the outside.

The Wales Tourist Board can provide the relevant information about all opening times of castles, plus what to do and see in Wales in general.

Wales Tourist Board
Brunel House
2 Fitzalan Road
Cardiff CF2 1UY
Tel: 01222 499909

Cadw
Brunel House
2 Fitzalan Road
Cardiff CF2 1UY
Tel: 01222 500200

National Trust
Trinity Square
Llandudno LL30 2DE
Tel: 01492 860123

National Trust
The King's Head
Bridge Street
Llandeilo SA19 6BN
Tel: 01558 822800

The castles are arranged in this book in alphabetical order.

Above: Cardiff Castle from Bute Park.

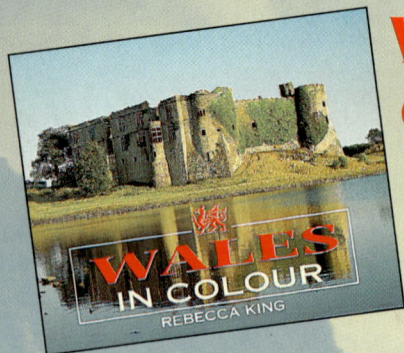

5
minute
DINOSAUR
STORIES

WRITTEN BY
Gabby Dawnay

ILLUSTRATED BY
Mona K

MAGIC CAT 🐱 PUBLISHING

In this book you'll find nine dinosaur stories
to read aloud, each one just 5 minutes long.

Each one is an adventure from the prehistoric world...
waiting to be discovered by you!

At the end of each story, explore an informative
'ALL ABOUT' page with a grown-up.

All about ANCHIORNIS

Anchiornis, whose name means 'near bird', lived around 160 MYA, in the Late Jurassic Period. These crow-sized carnivores were part of the Troodontidae family of bird-like theropod dinosaurs.

The plumage was mostly black and grey, with a head crest of reddish-brown feathers.

The front limbs were feathered and wing-like.

It's not entirely clear whether Anchiornis used its wings to flap or glide.

The hind legs may have been a second set of wings for gliding, or display, or both!

Sharp claws may have been used to climb trees as well as for gripping prey.

Like other theropods, Anchiornis had hollow bones and three clawed toes on each limb.

With feathers, wings and a beak full of sharp teeth, Anchiornis is an important part of the story of how birds evolved.

44

Which **5 minute** DINOSAUR STORY
will you read today?

Millions and millions of years long ago,
when the climate was hotter and harsh,
some animals crept from the soupy seas
and slowly climbed onto the marsh...

This is the story of dinosaurs -
from the beat of their feet to their feathers and claws,
to the food that they eat - was it veggie or meat?
Did they nibble or snap with their jaws?

From their scales to their tails,
some were small, some were tall,
some were toothy
and armoured
and strong...

TRIASSIC PERIOD
252-201 million
years ago

HEAR THEIR STORIES UNFOLD FROM THE BRAVE TO THE BOLD, EVERY ONE ONLY 5 MINUTES LONG!

The Age of the Dinosaurs

MESOZOIC ERA
(252-66 million years ago)

CRETACEOUS PERIOD
145-66 million
years ago

JURASSIC PERIOD
201-145 million
years ago

NYASASAURUS is FIRST on the SCENE

Long, long ago,
many years in the past,
lived a creature we know
moved incredibly fast.

While the stars shone above
and the world spun below,
she was born in Pangaea
a long time ago...

In the Middle Triassic -
not early, not late -
she was possibly first,
and the oldest to date.

Neither terribly heavy
nor terribly tall,
no, she didn't weigh much,
being truly quite small.

"I may not be big,
but I'm sturdy and strong. —
plus the length of my tail
is amazingly long!"

7

She moved super-quick,
being fast on her feet,
and she ran with a gang
of the dino-elite!

"We are small, but our legs
make us nimble and quick.
We can race round this place
like we're chasing a stick!"

Speedy and agile, with miniature claws,
a cousin – perhaps – of the first dinosaurs.

Nyasasaurus
(or 'Nya' for short)
always ran here and there,
"Because running's my sport!

"Who knows what's in store,
and whatever its name,
you need speed to survive
in the dinosaur game."

Each beautiful day,
as the Sun warmed the dew,
"Shall we race back to base?"
Nya called to her crew.

In the mist of the marsh
and the heat of the Sun,
"Shall we rush through the mush?"
Nya said, *"Let us run!"*

But maybe the thing
that made Nya a winner,
was how fast she ran
when her mama called… *"DINNER!"*

Oh, the hoot of the scoot
for the dinosaur dude
as she raced through the reeds
roaring, *"Let's get our food!"*

And will it be lizard
in bog-water soup?
Or a portion of flies
with a dollop of poop?

"Maybe some ferns
with a frog on the side?
Oh, the frogs in Triassic
are classic!" she cried.

With so much to guzzle,
and more to explore,
there are things we can puzzle
but cannot be sure…

Although she ran upright
and had a strong jaw,
was she really the first,
and a 'true dinosaur?'

And yes, *Nyasasaurus*
was fast on her feet–
but the question remains:
What on Earth did she eat?

All about NYASASAURUS

Nyasasaurus lived from about 245 to 240 million years ago (MYA). Many scientists believe it is the earliest known dinosaur. But they are studying its fossils to make sure it's a 'true dinosaur' and not a close relative. Either way, Nya is very old!

Dinosaurs roamed Earth for 170 million years, during a time called the Mesozoic Era (around 252-66 MYA). They first appeared 245 MYA in the Triassic Period.

Triassic archosaurs had a hole in the skull between the eye socket and the nostril.

Strong jaw muscles could open wide and clamp down with force.

They belong to an animal group known as archosaurs, which appeared near the start of the Triassic Period.

An upright stance with parallel legs sets dinosaurs apart from other reptiles.

Like other dinosaurs, Nyasasaurus laid eggs and lived on land.

Based on a few fossil bones, it is estimated Nyasasaurus weighed 20-60 kilograms and was 2-3 metres long from head to tail tip.

Goodbye to Nya and goodbye, Triassic.
Now things are about to get BIG in Jurassic...

STEGOSAURUS
is SLOW but SPiKY

Long, long ago
in the later Jurassic,
the world contained
even more dinosaur traffic.

As oceans and landmasses
started to grow,
many dinos evolved
to be awfully s-l-o-w…

Stegosaurus was one
and he moved at a speed
that was more of a stroll,
"'Cause a stroll's all I need!

"I enjoy taking time,
and I don't care at all
if my body is big
and my head is too small!"

His front legs were short,
but his back legs were longer.
"I'm built like a moveable fort —
but I'm stronger!"

He didn't like fighting
and answered to 'Stega'…
So famously mighty -
you might call him mega!

"I munch and I trudge
and I trudge and I munch,
vegetation for breakfast,
for dinner and lunch...

"And although I am slow,
as I move down the track,
I have spikes on my tail
and an armour-clad back!"

"My back is protected
by beautiful plates —
they are rigid and pointy,
a little like slates."

Oh, poor *Stegosaurus*...
Why, didn't you know
that your glorious plates
aren't protection, but show?

He doesn't - of course -
since his brain is so teeny.
Compared to his body,
it's tiny - it's weeny.

And here comes a carnivore,
stalking and sly.
"What is this that I see?
Can it be? Me oh my!

"Why, those scutes are too cute.
I have nothing to fear
from a silly old slow coach
like you – now come here!

"Lovely beast – you're a feast!
You're a plump, chewy snack!"
And at once Allosaurus
prepares to attack…

Watch out mega Stega!
You're sturdy and stout.
Walk away while you can,
'cause you can't run her out!

Stegosaurus was chill
but he could be quite sassy,
*"See, being a herbivore
does make me gassy..."*

The carnivore smiles while she says, *"Hello, lunch!"*
But then Steg takes a swipe and it sure packs a punch!

With a whacking great whoosh of his long, four-prong tail,
he has pumelled her back with a spike like a nail...

Steg isn't smart,
for his head is so small,
but he knows in his heart
that good timing is all!

All about STEGOSAURUS

Stegosaurus is probably the most famous member of the stegosaur family. These magnificently adorned dinos lived from about 170 to 100 MYA, in the Late Jurassic Period.

A blow from Stegosaurus's four-spiked tail could be deadly to attackers, such as Allosaurus.

Scutes (bony triangular plates) ran down the back and made Stegosaurus look bigger and fiercer. They may also have helped keep the dinosaur cool by evaporating heat.

This heavy, slow-moving herbivore (plant-eater) had a top speed of between 5 and 10 kilometres per hour.

The head was tiny compared to the rest of the body, and the brain was roughly the size of a lime.

Stegosaurus walked on four legs but the front two were much shorter than the back ones. The arrangement held up a heavy body of around 6,300 kilograms (similar to an African elephant!).

So much to discover
and more to be found,
with your head in the sky
and your feet on the ground...

BRACHIOSAURUS
is SO VERY TALL

The sunshine was beaming, the forest was green,
as a dinosaur strolled through the flourishing scene.

From the hush of the lush
to a jungle so dense,
comes the gentlest of giants –
gigantic, immense!

Because of the size
of her mountainous girth,
she has four solid legs
to support her on earth...

"Hello clouds, hello sky,
hello top of the wood —
I am tallest of all
and I feel mighty good!"

Ginkgoes, sequoias
and conifers vast,
gently swayed out the way
as the giant walked past.

"Oh, wonderful flora!
My forest of green,
where the plants are the greatest
you ever have seen!

"I'm a muncher, a cruncher,
an eating machine...
If it's leafy, it's lunch –
I'm the foliage queen!"

She is massively sturdy and terribly strong,
with a beautiful neck over 9 meters long!

"With my face in the clouds
I can breathe in the breeze,
as I nibble the buds
on the tops of the trees."

And sometimes, it's true
other creatures might stare,
asking questions like,

"How goes the weather up there...?"

"When your head is high up
and your body is vast,
it is hard to keep track
of the world going past..."

But imagine the marvel
of being this tall.
"I can stare at the clouds
and I study them all!

"With the sun on my face
in the cool of the air,
there is no finer place
on this Earth — anywhere!"

"From the tip of my tail
to the crown on my head,
see how smoothly I move
with my mountainous tread!"

She sniffs as she sways,
and can sense as she plods,
the familiar rumble
of MORE sauropods...

There's a shudder, a shake,
and a rumbling thud,
as the *Brachiosauruses*
march through the mud!

Every one has a back
like a smooth, hilly mound
and they graze where the
very best foliage is found.

With their heads in the clouds,
they delight in the breeze,
as they nibble the buds
on the tops of the trees.

Then they stare at the stars
and they dream of them all.
Oh, the towering wonder
of being so tall!

All about BRACHIOSAURUS

Brachiosaurus dinosaurs lived from about 155 to 140 MYA in the Late Jurassic Period. They were part a group of dinosaurs called sauropods - colossal, long-necked herbivores that walked on four legs.

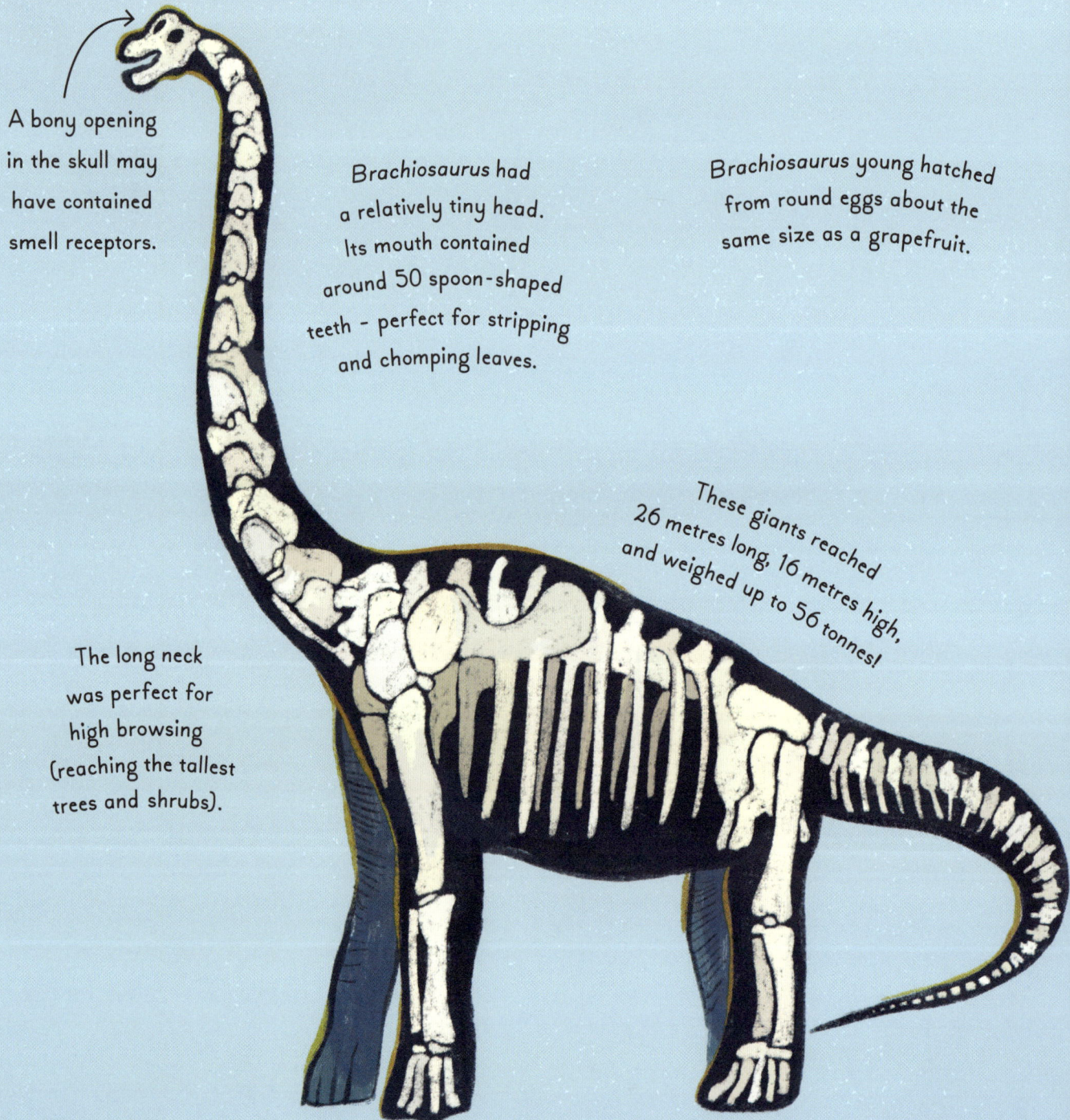

A bony opening in the skull may have contained smell receptors.

Brachiosaurus had a relatively tiny head. Its mouth contained around 50 spoon-shaped teeth - perfect for stripping and chomping leaves.

Brachiosaurus young hatched from round eggs about the same size as a grapefruit.

These giants reached 26 metres long, 16 metres high, and weighed up to 56 tonnes!

The long neck was perfect for high browsing (reaching the tallest trees and shrubs).

Its front legs were longer than its back legs, lifting its head even higher.

From giant and gentle,
to tiny and fierce...
Here's a dino with feathers
and claws that can pierce...

ANCHIORNIS
is SOARING on HIGH

With his feathers and beak,
it is not so absurd
to discover this dino
was almost a bird...

Anchiornis the dinosaur
may have been small,
but his coat made of feathers
was finest of all.

"With a black-and-grey body
and copper-red crest,
my plumage is perfect –
I'm simply the best!

"My powerful limbs
are especially long.
I am mightily flighty
and awfully strong!"

With sharp little claws,
he could climb up the trees
and then sweep through the sky,
riding high on the breeze...

So he lifts from a branch
and he goes with the flow,
drifting slowly, exploring
the forest below...

Using four feathered limbs,
he could hover and steer,
"Because I see the world
so much better from here...

"By gliding away
I am silent and slick...
What a wonderful way
to display such a trick!"

As he circles above,
he is searching beneath,
with his twinkling eyes
and a beak full of teeth.

"And although I have wings,
I will have to decide
if it's better to flap
or it's cooler to glide..."

Now a lizard is sunning
itself on the ground -
there's a *whoosh* from the sky
and a terrible sound...

With a flashing of feathers,
a swoop and a dash,
Anchiornis descends
but he lands with a...
CRASH!

The lizard escapes –
Anchiornis just shrugs.
"Oh, no matter!" he mutters,
"I'll gobble some bugs...

"If I tumble and fall
every once in a while,
well, you can't win them all!"
he declares with a smile.

"You see I am small,
but I'm simply the best,
from the claws on my toes
to my copper-red crest!"

So much to imagine and more to explore:
Did he fly using two wings - or possibly four?

Did he squeak? Did he roar?
Did he sing as he flew
across forest to shore?
Oh, if only we knew!

But with feathery wings, plus the things we can't see -
Anchiornis begins how the birds came to be...

All about ANCHIORNIS

Anchiornis, whose name means 'near bird', lived around 160 MYA, in the Late Jurassic Period. These crow-sized carnivores were part of the Troodontidae family of bird-like theropod dinosaurs.

The plumage was mostly black and grey, with a head crest of reddish-brown feathers.

It's not entirely clear whether *Anchiornis* used its wings to flap or glide.

The front limbs were feathered and wing-like.

The hind legs may have been a second set of wings for gliding, or display, or both!

Sharp claws may have been used to climb trees as well as for gripping prey.

Like other theropods, *Anchiornis* had hollow bones and three clawed toes on each limb.

With feathers, wings and a beak full of sharp teeth, *Anchiornis* is an important part of the story of how birds evolved.

Mysterious, marsh-dwelling,
kind of dramatic,
the next dino is spiny
and semi-aquatic...

SPINOSAURUS is SPINE-CHILLING

How lovely to live where the mangroves grow high,
in a tangle of roots as the water flows by...

But something is coming,
and even the sight
of his dazzling spine
and you'll faint out of fright!

He's bigger than *T. rex*,
who's not yet appeared.
Oh! This dino is thrilling,
he's spine-chilling – weird!

'Mysterio-saurus'
with razor-sharp teeth,
is the master of marshlands
and waters beneath.

He squelches through swamps
and he dwells on the coast,
for the salty green sea
is the place he loves most.

"What a wonderful feeling
to wade in the flood,
where my twinkle-toes sink
into soft, squashy mud!"

He's called *Spinosaurus*
because of his spine –
a spectacular fan
that's exceedingly fine!

The curving addition
attached to his back,
makes him seem extra-large
if he needs to attack.

And once in the water,
you see how his frill
is a warning to all
that he's out for a kill.

*"The frill keeps me chill
and it acts like a sign,
but the way that it waves
in the wind is divine!"*

Those crocodile teeth whisper, *"I have a wish, from the ocean beneath I will catch me a fish!"*

Sporting his sail-top he steers through the waves with a rudder-like tail, hunting fishes – his faves!

He lurks in the slipstreams and shadows a while, where he licks every tooth of his crocodile smile.

"YIKES!" cry the fishes,
"That dino is sneaky.
He looks mighty fine but
his snout is so...beaky!"

There's a dash and a splash
as a shadow swims past
in a flickering flash –
it is big – it is fast!

This fish is a slick one
and turns with a flicker –
its movements are quick...
Spinosaurus is quicker.

He rises triumphant –
it's not a surprise
that he holds in his jaws
a magnificent prize.

Then everyone sighs,
and some others grow pale.
"Oh, what wonderful spines!"
They declare, "What a sail!"

"So handsome and mighty,"
they cry, "and so proud!"
Spinosaurus is mobbed
by a passionate crowd…

"Oh my, Spinosaurus –
just look at your spine!
That spectacular fan
is exceedingly fine!"

He scoots through the sea and they swoon with delight –
for his glorious frill is a spine-chilling sight!

All about SPINOSAURUS

Spinosaurus was a large, carnivorous theropod that lived from about 99 to 94 MYA in the Late Cretaceous Period. It measured 14 metres from nose to tail-tip and weighed 7,400 kilograms - about the same as the famously fearsome *Tyrannosaurus rex*.

Its sail made *Spinosaurus* look bigger, and may have regulated body temperature. It is possible that males had more elaborate sails to attract mates.

It had short legs and a wide, paddle-like tail.

The teeth had sharp, cone-shaped points, similar to those of a modern crocodile.

Spinosaurus spent lots of time near water, but scientists continue to debate whether it was a fast swimmer or more of a wader.

Spinosaurus lived in swampy marshlands and along rivers. It is the largest carnivorous dinosaur known (so far) and it and its cousins are the only ones that may have lived a semi-aquatic life.

Next an odd bird of prey,
like a thief in the night.
Run away if you can,
or prepare for a fight...

VELOCIRAPTOR
has a KILLER CLAW

Something is stirring
and searching about,
with her two beady eyes
and her long, toothy snout...

The fabulous creature
you'll meet in this chapter
is dapper and deadly,
she's *Velociraptor*!

She is sassy and small,
she's feathered and quick,
with a sickle-like claw
that is basically sick!

This dino is skillful
at pinning and stabbing
with two crescent claws
that are perfect for grabbing.

"I'm fancy-pants Velo,
just look how I strut,
with my hooks in the air
and my feathery butt!"

Two muscular legs
help her scoot over sands
and her swaggering style
is well-known in these lands.

"You'll see me and GASP,
for my strike is sublime.
I don't pause with these claws,
so I win every time."

She's a charmer, you know,
with her colourful wings
that are only for show,
and not flighty-type things...

"Many feathers have I —
but oh no, I don't fly,
for I never lift off,
even though I might try!

"My feathers are warming -
my feathers delight...
Oh, my feathers protect me
but DON'T give me flight!"

She sprints for a while,
turning into a clearing,
her long-feathered tail
giving balance and steering.

"Now my tummy is rumbling —
I'm after a BITE.
Say 'hello' to my claws,
'cause it's time for a FIGHT!"

She jumps with delight as her dinner runs past,
and quickly she pins it then hooks to hold fast!

"I'm a smooth operator!
A brawler – a baiter,
with teeth like a 'gator to...
eat you up later!

"I'm fancy-pants Velo.
Just look how I strut,
with my hooks in the air
and my feathery butt."

"As I swagger along
with my confident walk,
I will sing you a song
that sounds more like a squawk...

CRAW! CRAW!
HEE-HAWW!

"I'm dapper but deadly,
and sure, I'm adored,
being famously feathered
and scarily clawed!"

The size of a turkey
but never your friend…
She will eat you for supper,
you see, in the end.

All about VELOCIRAPTOR

Velociraptor was a carnivorous (meat-eating) dinosaur living from about 74 to 70 MYA in the Cretaceous Period. This swift-moving predator could run at speeds of up to 40 kilometres an hour.

Velociraptor had feathers and mini-wings, but could not fly. It stood half a metre high (about the size of a turkey), and behaved like a flightless eagle.

The long, feather-covered tail helped with balance and steering at high speeds.

It likely made squawking noises similar to a modern bird of prey.

Feathers were for warmth and protection, and may have been brightly coloured to attract mates.

Strong, muscular legs

The middle toe of each three-toed foot had a 6.5 centimetre-long sickle-shaped claw. It was used to grab, stab, hook and pin down (rather than slash).

The talon on the second toe was held off the ground to keep it razor-sharp.

With a boom and a bash,
then a crash and a roar,

it is time to discover
the king dinosaur...

TYRANNOSAURUS REX
is the KING CARNIVORE

Sixty-six million Earth years ago,
lived a dinosaur king that you probably know...

A terrible *T. rex*
with two beady eyes,
looking this way and that
for a tasty surprise.

"I'm a megastar monarch — the best of the best.
I'm the mightiest beast and I feast on the rest!"

A tyrant tyrannosaur breaking the laws
with his flesh-ripping fangs in his bone-crushing jaws.

"I'm T. rex the Terrible!
Look at my bite –
every herbivore here
will be dying of fright!"

Sniffing for lunch
with his powerful snout,
he is licking his lips
as he wanders about.

From the meat in his teeth
to the curve of his claw,
there is death on the breath
of the king carnivore.

Not too far away
at the edge of the glade,
an *Edmontosaurus*
had stopped in the shade…

He basks in a bower
and mutters, *"Superb!"*
As he nibbles a flower
and guzzles a herb.

The air seems to hum
with the scent of the blooms,
as they mingle and mix
in a thousand perfumes.

*"The blossoms round here
are deliciously sweet.
Every fern, every plant
is a herbivore treat!"*

With so much to munch,
he is too busy working
to pick up the scent
of a carnivore lurking.

With a rustle, a crackle
and suddenly–*SNAP!*
It seems *Edmontosaurus*
walked into a trap…

Oh, beware - oh, beware
of a T. rex, *"Surprise!"*
From the death on his breath,
to the glint in his eyes.

"Dinner at last,"
thunders Rex. *"I can tell!*
With my terrible nose
and its top sense of smell!"

But running around
under blossoming trees,
the *T. rex* was starting
to tickle and wheeze…

And while he is running
to see what he's caught,
he explodes with a sneeze
that is more like a… SNORT!

By now he is huffing and puffing his jaws,
as he flaps all around with his miniature paws.

Yes, Rex was the boss
and a ruler supreme,
reigning millions of years
in a deadly regime.

A tyrant tyrannosaur
breaking the laws
with his flesh-ripping fangs
in his bone-crushing jaws.

"But even a T. rex
can have a bad day,"
says *Edmontosaurus*,
while sprinting away...

All about TYRANNOSAURUS REX

Tyrannosaurus rex lived in the Late Cretaceous Period from about 68 to 66 MYA. This large, carnivorous dinosaur was one of the most fearsome and famously successful predators of all time.

Its name means 'king of the tyrant lizards', from the Greek words *tyranno* ('tyrant') and *saurus* ('lizard') with the Latin word *rex* ('king').

T. rex had three times the biting power of a modern lion and a keen sense of smell.

T. rex walked upright on strong back legs. Scientists remain unsure about what its tiny, muscular arms were used for!

The bone-crushing jaws contained 60 serrated teeth, each 20 centimetres in length.

Tyrannosaurus rex lived just as lush, flowering plants like magnolias and hydrangeas were beginning to appear...

...but did this fearsome carnivore get hayfever? No one knows!

With a trio of horns
and a marvellous beak,
just imagine the tales
if this dino could speak...

TRICERATOPS is TERRIBLY TOUGH

Adorned like a queen with a frill made of bone,
along comes *Triceratops*, solid as stone...

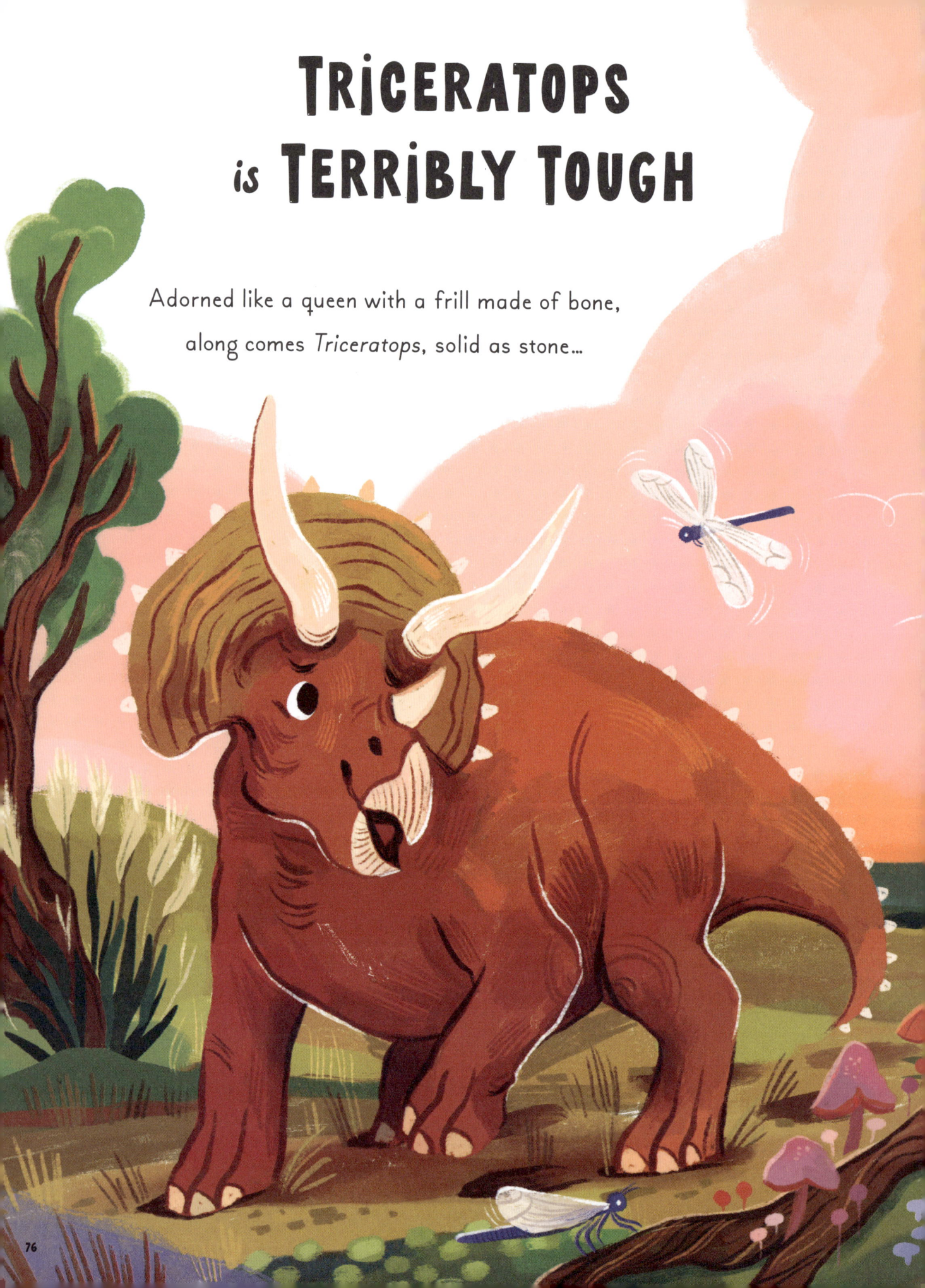

"I know I look fierce,
and I'm clearly immense,
but the armour I wear
is, of course, self-defence.

"'Three horns' is my name,
so it's true to suppose,
I have two on my head
and a third on my nose."

She plods through the bogs
on a path of her own.
She is big, she is strong,
but entirely alone...

A lonely *Triceratops*
walking along
with her three lovely horns
sings a sorrowful song.

"Is it wrong to feel sad as I stroll through the green?
Is it really so bad that I want to be seen?"

Triceratops thinks, 'How I wish I could speak
to another like me with a parrot-like beak.'

Slowly she nibbles
some palms in the wood.
"*These are terribly tough,
but the taste is so good.*"

She chews on a leaf and
she says, "*Why, oh why,
am I all on my own?
I am lonely, am I!*"

Then she munches a fern,
and she munches some more
as she listens and waits,
but for what, she's not sure.

79

Triceratops stops
in the shade of a tree.
And she calls to her crew,
"Where, oh where can they be?"

Until here comes a fellow
with glittering eyes
and a mouth full of teeth,
winking, 'What a surprise!'

"Hello there, I'm T. rex!"
he cries, "I'm a winner!
You look very lonely –
please join me for dinner?"

Don't do it *Triceratops*! Maybe you're sad,
but a date with a *T. rex*? Don't do it – he's bad!

Then Rex opens his jaws,
crying, *"I want a snack!"*
With a thunderous roar,
he prepares to attack.

Triceratops gulps
without making a sound.
But she stares at the *T. rex*
while holding her ground.

*"My frill is protection,
but look at my horns...
they are long, they are strong
and they're POINTY!"* she warns.

"I'm sorry", he stutters,
"Alone, you are charming.
But now I can see that
as more, you're...alarming!"

And the lonely-no-longer *Triceratops* cries,
"At last, my dear friends — what a sight for sore eyes!"

All about TRICERATOPS

Triceratops lived at the same time as *T. rex*, from about 68 to 66 MYA, in the Late Cretaceous Period. At 9 metres long and weighing 14,000 kilograms, it was a big herbivore.

Triceratops had two large horns above its eyes, used mostly as defence against predators, and one small nose horn.

A big, bony frill protected the neck and may also have regulated body temperature.

There is some evidence that young Triceratops spent time in groups, but most of them were solitary dinosaurs.

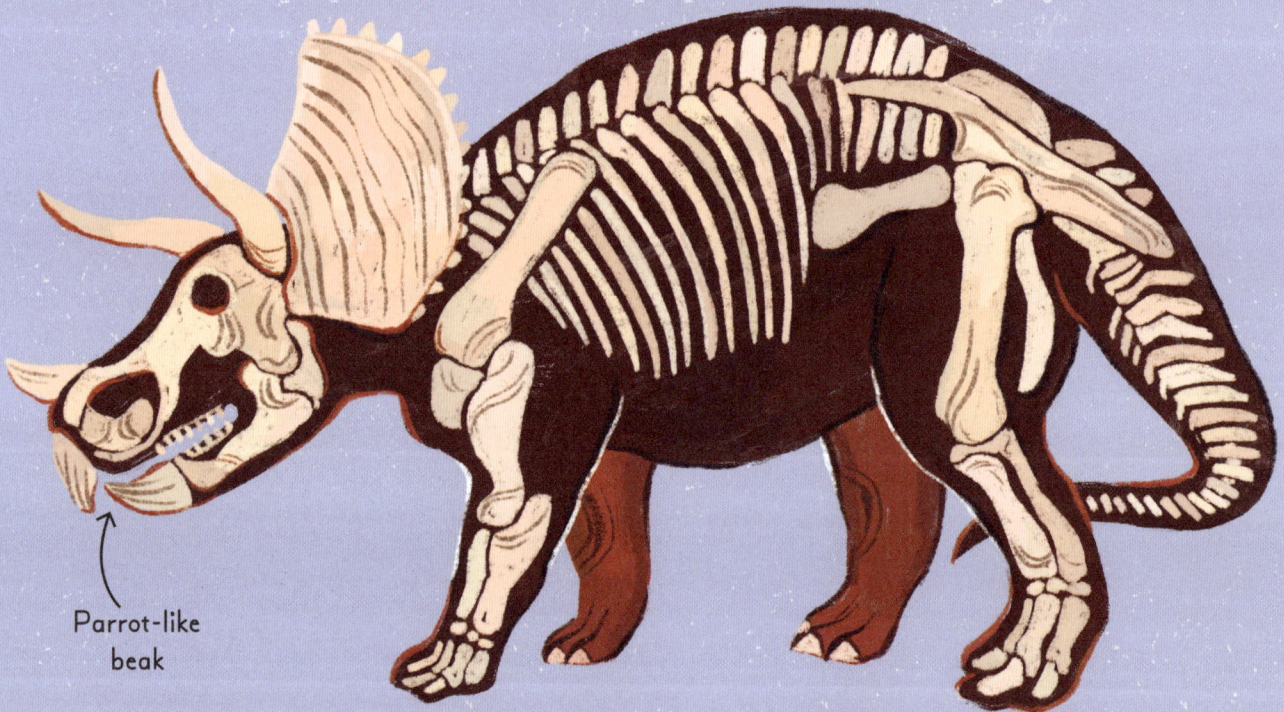

Parrot-like beak

The 800 teeth were arranged in rows. They were continually worn down by stripping tough vegetation and replaced.

Although one of T. rex's main meals, *Triceratops* would have used its horns to fight back. And it seems likely that a T. rex might think twice if facing a small group rather than a single *Triceratops*!

Club-wielding, armoured –
oh, what have we here?
Just a leaf-munching herbivore –
nothing to fear!

ANKYLOSAURUS
is ARMED and READY

Something is moving along on the track,
with a helmet-like head and an iron-clad back...

Protected by armour
from head down to toe,
he is sturdy and steady
and ready to go!

"More than four thousand kilos,
and nine metres long,
I am low-slung and slow,
but incredibly strong.

"I am chunky and clumpy,
my armour's intense,
and a wag of my tail
is the best self-defence..."

It's Ankylosaurus!
A plate-covered dude
with a tail like a club
and a craving for food.

He doesn't mind much
if it's leafy or sticky –
a low-growing fern
or a fruit – he's not picky.

"I might dig around in the ground for a root,

"or keep grazing above for the juiciest shoot."

"From fibrous to barky,
I try every plant.
Sometimes prickles are tricky
but never say, 'Can't!'"

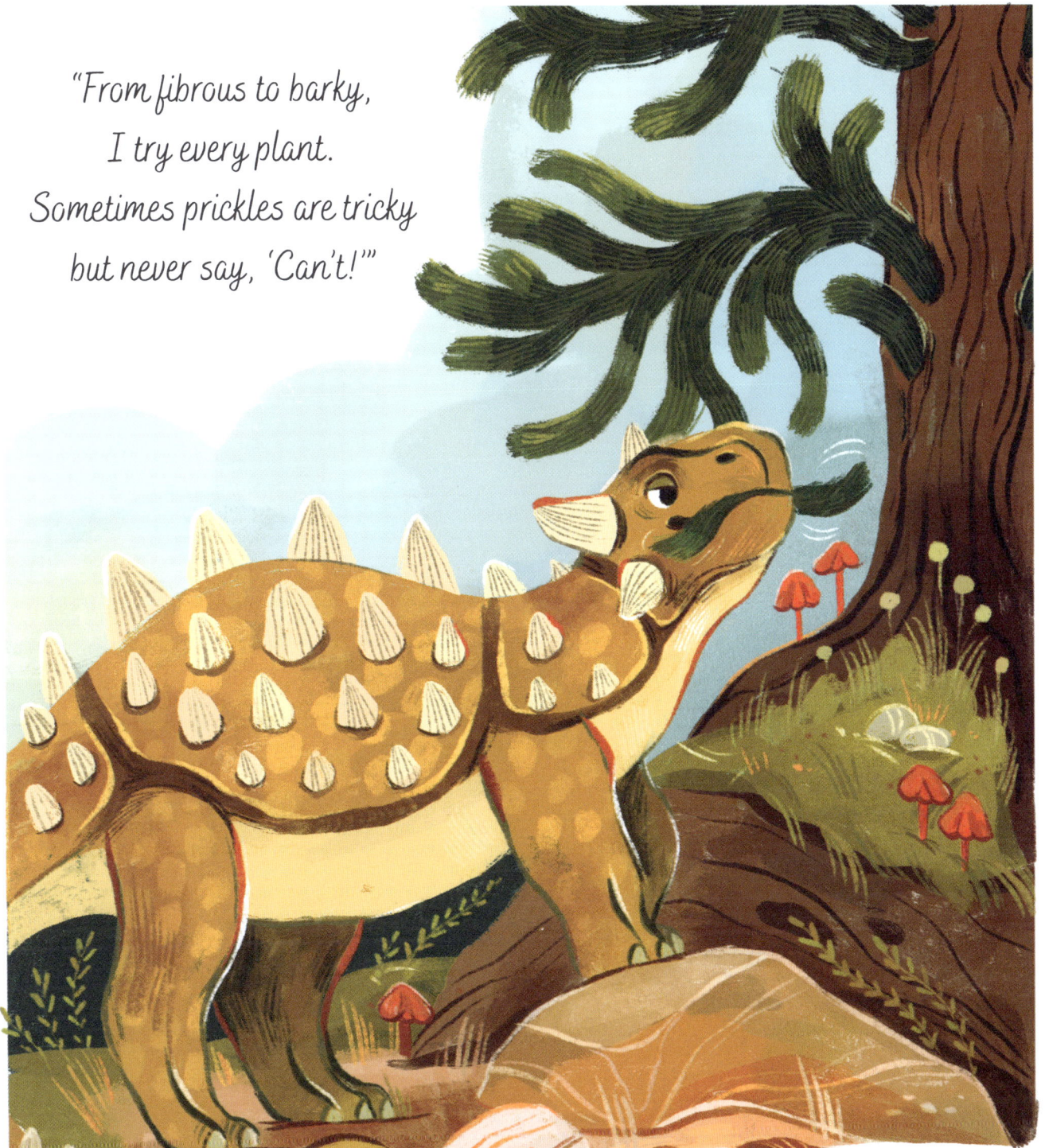

He stops for a moment
to sniff at some trees,
and he breathes in a scent
drifting by on the breeze...

An odour so lovely,
a fragrance so sweet,
that it must come from
something delicious to eat.

He follows the smell
with his powerful nose,
'til he reaches a flower
the shape of a rose.

*"A sugar magnolia.
Oh, what a taste!
Much too pretty to eat,
far too tasty to waste!"*

Of course, this digester
of foliage and flower
can turn vegetation
from pretty to power!

Ankylosaurus
is taking a bite,
when he smells something else –
and it doesn't smell right.

With a mouth full of petals
he stands by the shrub,
then he steadies himself,
and he readies his club...

As a *T. rex* appears
from the dark of the wood,
"I can see," Anky whispers,
"this fellow's no good!"

There's a walloping whistle…
A WHOOSH! Then a THWACK!
As the club lands a blow
on the predator's back…

Now the *T. rex* is waving
his two tiny paws,
crying *"STOP!"* at the top
of his terrible jaws.

"I am the KING!"
roars the T. rex, "OK?!
But you've won. I'm done in...
for the third time this day!

"And I quit — this is it...
I am GOING AWAY!"

Ankylosaurus

is slow as a snail.

"But you'd better watch out
for the SLUG of my tail!"

All about ANKYLOSAURUS

Ankylosaurus lived from about 68 to 66 MYA in the Cretaceous Period. Along with *Stegosaurus*, it was part of a dinosaur group called Thyreophora, which means 'shield bearer'. This herbivore was the ultimate 'armoured tank' dinosaur – heavy and slow moving but super-protected.

Perhaps they really did enjoy smelling (and eating) magnolias, the first of which appeared more than 100 MYA, making them one of the oldest flowering families on Earth!

Bony, keratin-coated plates covered the body.

Ankylosaurus consumed around 60 kilograms of plant matter every day! It wasn't fussy and would likely try any low-growing vegetation it came across. It may have even used its two front legs to dig for roots.

The heavy, club-shaped tail swayed from side to side as Ankylosaurus walked, and was mainly for defence, rather than attack.

Being a herbivore did not mean Ankylosaurus was harmless. Just like modern hippos, rhinos and elephants, they could be aggressive and would certainly have been dangerous to mess with.

Dinosaurs roamed
and they ruled over all
because dinosaurs ROCK,
from the big to the small!

FURTHER READING

The Fossil Keeper's Treasure by Amy Atwater

Lift the Flap: Encyclopaedia of Dinosaurs by Eryl Nash

My Grandparents Were Dinosaurs by Anne and Steve Brusatte

For the eager diggers and excavators with a passion for times long past,
may your curiosity never go extinct!
– Mona K

For all the dinosaur fans out there, keep exploring and learning... As palaeontologist
Richard Fortey (1946-2025) said, "Dinosaurs remind us that the world is full of
mysteries waiting to be discovered, and curiosity is the key to unlocking them."
– Gabby D

MAGIC CAT PUBLISHING

5 Minute Dinosaur Stories © 2026 Lucky Cat Publishing Ltd
Text © 2026 Gabby Dawnay
Illustrations © 2026 Mona K
First Published in 2026 by Magic Cat Publishing, an imprint of Lucky Cat Publishing Ltd,
Unit 2 Empress Works, 24 Grove Passage, London E2 9FQ, UK

A catalogue record for this book is available from the British Library.

ISBN 978-1-917366-26-7

The illustrations were created using gouache, coloured pencil and digital media
Set in Bakerie, Claytonia, Pistachio and Quicksand

Published by Rachel Williams and Jenny Broom
Edited by Rosie Neave
Designed by Ashtyn Botterill
Consulted by Steve Brusatte

Manufactured in China

9 8 7 6 5 4 3 2 1

FSC
www.fsc.org
MIX
Paper | Supporting
responsible forestry
FSC® C104723

Also available: